ROOM 140

MITCHELL KATO

Outskirts Press, Inc.
http://www.outskirtspress.com

ISBN: 978-1-9772-5296-8

Outskirts Press and the "OP" logo are trademarks belonging to Outskirts Press, Inc.

PRINTED IN THE UNITED STATES OF AMERICA

A study on a universal

Room140 is where
I was told
Good is not to be done.

Table of Contents

Part One
(drawings)

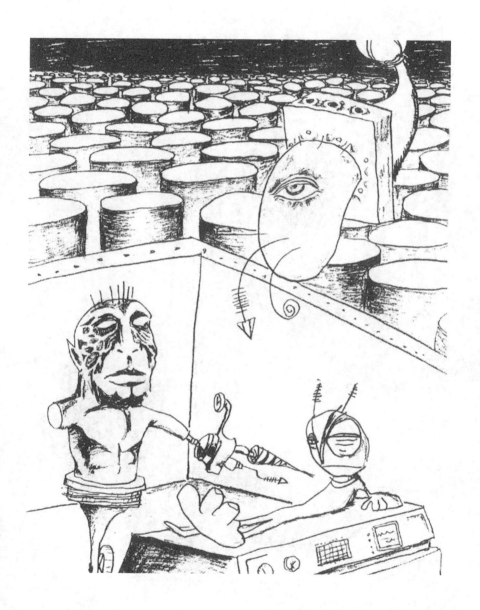

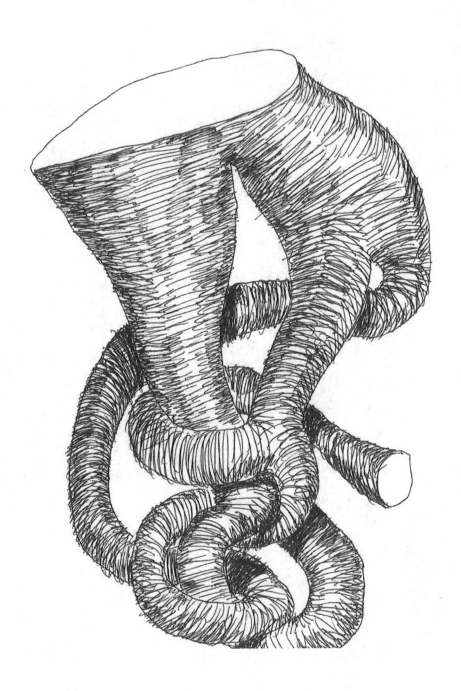

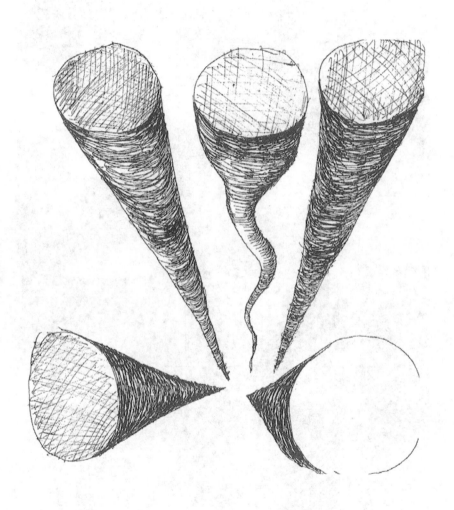

PART TWO
(POEMS)

And Circle, Square, Triangle

*****

the writers like
Dostoevsky makes much
of nothing. in fact, out of mud.
manuscript travels across the land
and readers make life of bitter
letters---lets make them Russian dance.

*****

the art collector
he come across the country to see this
virgin painting.
he has seen painting many has seen. But this one is exquisite.
He (the collector) has unsaddled from the horse
the painter rushes to him and kiss his hand (what a drama)
because he is truly a patron
and together they look at the painting.

*****

eternal recurrence is where He lives.
in fact, that makes him be something else.
that is to say, in a psychological state
only the dedicated viewer, only the secret one
perhaps a groundless, one claims the
logistic of Art.

*****

winter artist

he knows no pleasure
his finger touches ice
he thinks of his teachers
he thinks of his friends.
but what of this winter end
proof of his life.

*****

waste is king of progress

one action does not force of another action.
So there will be many power, many action to start
Yet, there can be something else as well
which should be called king freedom.

*****

the curator has the eye for the
painting. perhaps she has small eyes
the rest of civilization does not understand
the value of the painting.
in fact, the rest of the viewers
catch up to the art at the end of the time.
again, the fine logic of civilization
is introduced by the curator.

*****

curators are people who will be
awed by the paintings; a monument of a painting
and prostrate many times.
they will whisper to the artist
about matter only they will appreciate
after all who understands a painting
in words.

*****

in order to find the Painting
the artist travels.
different thoughts different places
different people
the artist will abandon All

and the artist will find
a special kind of Hope.

****

the most abstract is the curator

they do not associate with the rich
they have too much money

they do not associate with the artists
they are a bit too eccentric

so they are left with the paintings itself

they laugh with the paintings
they cry with the paintings
its worthy to protect all the art.

*****

the artists paints the content.
the frames are there for existence

*****

from the artists' fingers
to the curator's eyes
auctioneers' hammer
to the buyer's accountant
and to the interior designer
new family's living room.

the child looks up to the painting and the color of sunshine

*****

I am weak in my weakness
a pathetic condition; a dismal condition
my finger nerve is barely operational
medicated with brain drugs
all the other humans are strong in their strength
they say they are also strong in their weakness
and wiggling of the brush bluntly says so much

*****

feminist curator2

as she turns around in her
long grey hair in air
as you are waiting for an
advice of herbs
and she has story of friends
and events.
She is much older than you are
But she doesn't mind
She sniffs of her soup...

Then after a while of taping
Swinging fingers around
and an old fashion
hum:
"I guess I can't help you there..."

****

Feminist curator

she has long grey hair in air
experienced in life
in fact she hides from the
everyday world.
she has few friends
her room is with twisted opinion
her hands are language
that means nothing
hiding from the world

esoteric philosophy and
erotic movements
as the planets gives her
ancient knowledgeof difference
she has friends
only in the circle of
secret society of female priests

*****

pop art and candy politics

sure pop art killed abstract expressionism
while framing is the heart of
postmodern. if you can frame it
its post-modern art.
nothing deep about it.
like candy you can buy it
at the corner drug store.

And banana, Warhol, and Velvet Underground...

the "now" doesn't mean much
because when the moment comes when
you pop in the candy in the mouth.

and these days children got the fastest
and current video games.

*****

Mr. Twain

He has painted
Painted of bad luck
his master is Mark Twain
kept in dark for ages
it was the in between of luck
(and bad luck)
called luck-ology.
Americans are the only ones
to practice.

*****

Curator with hundred art pieces

Now that i think of it. The curator is the frame
And the artist himself is the art

*****

The Taoist

He pose the frame
The frame is Nature
It extends to the world.

And the master framer
Are all mathematicians

Super Science Fiction Thoughts

mathematics is model
physics (science) is the an application of models
philosophy is text itself.

This is what the fatherCyborg might have said:
1) One is Two.
2) Parmenides rejects Two.
3) good is a good act it brings the society together.
4) evil is a evil act. It divides the society.
5) Evil is when the universe ends.
6) Good is when the in entire Evil history is destroyed.
7) The Not is the kernel of cyborg brain.
8) Time is the bliss of the Church.
9) The Three is the present.
10) The law of trichotomy: the past, the present, and the future.
11) Reason is the tragedy of humans and the high priest of the Church.
12) The Not will be found where the philosophical cyborgs will finish his thoughts.
13) Parmenides is the orthodox One.
The following is disputed by the Church
14) The motherRobot will be almost Evil (but not true Evil, only asymptomatic.)
15) Silence is the song of the universe.
16) The three body problem is the thought of humans (Most likely the only theory of Humans.)
17) The Church holds absolute power with their contiunally adjusting big-bang clock.
18) And the renegades continually elude Church in their future.
19) The Church is always in conflict with JC and Reason. ("JC" is the scientific notion. Jesus Christ is the Christian Notion.)

20) There are true Jesus and false Jesus. And the false Jesus is as equal to true Jesus.

21) Some say, Homer was the last of the philosopher. I [fatherCyborg] say Heidegger was the last (Heidegger0).

A) The statement is either true or false.

B) Statement A can be complicated.

C) Reason

The messenger from the Pope calmed down the tention on the planet of grey.

1) Humans

2) motherRobot

3) cyborgs

4) golem

5) Scums

22) Luxury Citizen must put all efforts in to developing luxury arts.

23) The present art (modernism) must reflex the medium and the artist perspective of the world.

24) Classical art is the investigation of the reason of the art and the past reason of the art.

25) The future of art on the one hand is propaganda, on the other hand cultural criticism.

a) Language Correctness is the defender not only of syllogism but also the moral narratives.

b) The Writers' society is all and only about Freedom.

c) The motherRobot's priority is progress.

d) The fatherCyborg forecasts and controls the mental weather of the known universe.

26) The Church defends the idiosyncrasy of the world as much as JC is anomolous.

27) HEGEL was an earthly individual but also a cosmic existence.

28) Thales the Greek was the closest to human source and human thought.

29) The Church does not demand the motherRobot and cyborgs

to have faith in Jesus Christ because they can't (It is scientifically proven). Therefore, the Church only demands that only they believe in the scientific JC.

*****Eleven Commandments i can think of

1) the structure of language corresponds to the structure of the world. (Aristotle)
2) the problem of philosophy is the problem of language. (Anglo-America analytic school)
3) more particular more universal (me)
4) the subjective knowledge can be certain while objective knowledge is approximate. (me)
5) existence before essence (J.P. Sartre)
6) Thales "everything is water"; Parmenides "One"; Heraclitus "change"
7) HEGEL's dialectic: thesis, anti-thesis, synthesis
8) everything has a reason / there are no ultimate reason (Kant / Hume)
9) all statements are statements wherever the source is.
10) to know Good is to do Good.(Plato)
11) philosophy is therapy

Zen and the Art of Nuclear War

*

Isn't it exciting?
after the initial protocol
we fuel the missiles
we watch the hatch to open
we get the coded message
we push the red button
and we shoot the warheads to
far away
where it will be called
Hell.

*

Most people do not know the power
for them the earth is a flat parallel
never new will happen
But there are children who see
the signs
the brain wave of the people
One/Two/Three
and the earth will become a fireball.

*

HARAKIRI nuclear war

Who can nuke their own
country first with glory.

*

Things always have reasons.
But what if we do things just

to test if the world is paying attention.
May be you have thought a way
for "nuclear destruction"
You shove it in the big blue metal post
box, and look away,
whistle, and walk away.

*

Mental Illness of Nuclear Missile Phobia

Ahhhh
A man is screaming in the middle of the
road.
He says the nuclear missiles are coming.
"He has a problem of nuclear war".
the man next to me says.
I get on the bus.

*

How the mentally ill feels.
Do A or Nuclear War.
Don't do A. It's a blackmail.

1
*

Science of Man
changed with cold war
We are now, so serious
Even in play, we cannot let
the individual stray far.
We are intense about our
occupation and for living
we follow the leader.

Newton, although still true
are
demoted in favor of ecology.
As I said the individual cannot
leave the ecological system.
Our brains, we hold it up with our
hands. So it will not crack a part.
For maybe, the brain will be nuclear.

*

One of these day, we will be
so board that nuclear war
will happen just for
entertainment.
It does really matter if man
lives or not (or Hell or not.)

*

Nuclear War Anxiety Attack (a.k.a. NWAA)

It can happen anytime, anywhere, I just had
one in the grocery store.
And watch out, you might have
one when you are driving.

*

The American helicopters are like flowers

And the suffering of Zen master are not
real anymore. Because
The American generals, they bully.
They got the nuclear eyes.

*

roommate soaked in rain.
I give him a big hug and
in the rain he smiles.

*

The code for the nuclear missile launch
are actually poems.
The computer appreciates that. 15

*

What is the sound of one nuclear missle flying?

all nuclear missles flying.
0
*

With a gun, one may not able to
hit a small target.
But with a nuke, if you have it handy,
one cannot miss any target.

*

Deterrent Strategy for the Global Nuclear War

The stranger came. He said he was sent from
future of nuclear holocaust. He said he and others
live underground. He said he did not come to change
anything. He was going to write a poem which will make
no difference any ways.

*

What about a local nuclear bomb?
or what about the final bomb?

We might think if we drop the big bomb
it will destroy the other side of the earth.
So we will be safe. (even though we will share
the aftermath holocaust weather.) But another
question? Can we make a bomb strong enough
to crack the earth in pieces?

*

We made atheism so that atheists can make
the bombs. Truly the creators of the Bombs
are devils.
Though we could also think we made the Bomb
so we can get together in a different way.
Its a deterrent of actual war of the super powers.

*

In medieval times we had the language of
heaven/hell which was simple.
Now we have the language of
nuclear war/ technological utopia. which
is the complication of
computers and mental illness.

*

With the cold war we have a new type of
human beings. And we are waiting for the
coming of the Gods.

*

Atomic Man

No he does not get a super power from atoms.
When the time comes, he will be the

one who approaches the president who
is dying making the decision. The Atomic Man
will approach the president
"Here, I will push that red button for you."

*

There are two types of people. One type
does not mean anything. The other type
means things literally. Now, the literal type
hide in a stronghold. They got food. They
got weapons.

*

Buddhism is what Buddhist practice.
There are no Buddhist principles.
There are no Buddhist statements.
These days only the potential for
nuclear war is the only thing that moves
them.
(which is almost anything.)

*

The sound of electric buzz, high tech machinery
airplanes, and helicopters
takes me to the operation of the nuclear silos.

*

The gigantic intellectual who designed the
Nuclear Warfare Strategy Plan for the
computer (his only friend).
He watches all the humans in his life.
He applies his Plan to them.
An enormous game theory matrix, the only way
he can relate to others.

*

Poet of bomb lives in the in between:
The superficial surface of the humans,
and the bombed out world of fire.

*

We had a song called "bomb the world".
But no one let us play it in public.
One time we did play it, I believe, they
shut down the cozy open mic the next week

*

The computer has
demonstrated that
nuclear war is useless,
long time ago.
But humans were never
satisfied with that.
So, the generals kept
asking the same question:
how to win the nuclear war
----over and over.

*

There is a mathematical
proof that shows why we will
not have a nuclear war.
Except that it depends on
Axiom of Reason, which is
completely tortuous for man
to understand.

*

Hume (the Scottish skeptic philosopher) will be
sarcastically laughing of our statistics.
Do we think nuclear war is statistically
unavoidable? That the past will repeat in the future
and the statistics is the reliable indicator?
Or should we just eliminate all the statisticians
(with their software package)?
Send out assassins and kill them one by one.

*

I hope, Jesus, Buddha, Mohammed, Lao-Tsu,
Confucius were all aliens. Someone in this
space must have answers. Humans don't have answers. Hope
aliens do.

*

Reason and the death of human should not go
together, but who knows.
Somewhere, sometime, someone, for some reason
drops the bomb. But I say it will take
two days to overcome the shock. Everyone will
abandon the cities. The farmers will fortify their
farm. The city people in small town will have
their laptops. Then everyone will be calm. The
coast will flood because of the global warming.
I wonder what will happens to the astronauts?

*

Of course, we want to make a divide between
scientific language and ordinary language.

(Not so easy.)

Perhaps scientific language will tell us that
we, might as well, blow up all human beings
rather than needless medical suffering.
(Or who should we protect.)
It used to be, scientific language was the
privileged language. Now the ordinary language.

(The American political language.)
seems here the last say
(in this country.)

*

Individual suicide should not be allowed, as much as
the complete destruction of humankind should not
be allowed.

*

I know a real Buddhist. He is not troubled by nuclear bombs.
If he doesn't see it, if he doesn't speak it, the bombs
don't exist.
He slams the door shut.

*

Nuclear Bomb Testing

Maybe we should let the squirrels do it.
As it is we been doing the test on a curve
for such a long time that we are getting lazy.
Or would dogs do the job. They been pets
they got lazy too.
What about letting the Japanese beetles do the
task. No, they are too patriotic.
The moral of the story is that we are cooked
even at the stage of testing.

*

We are already living in a holocaust of ideas.
Humans are all nothing in their mind.
I stand and watch these poor humans who
got nowhere to go to find the ideas for them.
And I cannot make a move because I am full of
pride.

*

When a Buddhist steps off an airplane in
some Western city, he becomes non-Buddhist.
When a Buddhist shake hands with a non-Buddhist he becomes
non-Buddhist.
When a Buddhist writes a book of
Buddhist in a Western language its not a book about Buddhism.

*

Soon the Japanese Buddhist will be reading
translated American Buddhist literature.
And they will hide the books under their tatami. 8

Mentally Ill 543

*

Asylum is a type of abyss.
It reminds one that we are mentally ill.
There are no behavior of insane.
Its all very awkward.
And when one walks out of the hospital
one begins to live again
 (still handicapped.

*

There is not a one single thing about mental illness.
Except that often they have excessive anxiety.
And a large hospital bill.
And I still suck on my thumb (not really).
And I imagine myself to be the messiah of the intellectual.
And the future is coming, like it or not.
And I will make one million dollars sometime.
And I like the movie 12 monkeys.
And I am going to continue writing.
And I will live for a long long time.

*

infinity is hard to think of
and doing arithmetic with it
is also hard (think of the
power operation.)
to think infinity is to
fight with the compulsion.
it eludes all numbers.

*

My brother was a monkey.
And I was in my mother's lap.
When my parents fight, I suck on my thumb.
And me and my brother show off our toys to
each other.
Isn't it a happy day?

*

cringing away from what I must do.
what is against truth?
He is leaning over me.
Am I being immature?
But I thought I was an iconoclast.
I thought I always do what
I want to do.

What is the world, if I must do what
I must not do?

*

set of all natural numbers are infinity of language
set of space-time is the infinity of the world.
now is there a infinity in between the two?

*

Time goes only forward.
So, that's good.

One acquirers things.
One throw away things.
One must make decisions
about things,
always,

So, that's hard.

*

schizophrenics

They foresee decline
so the soul divides
into plurality.

*

N.T.

This poem is not about
the New Testament,
but it should be noted that
the New Testament is
motivated by Love.
Now, N.T. is my therapist.
She might be also motivated by Love,
I don't know.
But as a schizophrenic I wonder
what I am motivated by?
A defeated Truth that is not willing
to die just yet.

*

There is a king in this library.
But he does not budge me.
I am a black fly
That does not rhyme
well.

*

Doing your job twice in
a day, is a vice.
And there are no perfection
you tell yourself.
There have been harder
days.
This is when work is done by the
mind.

*

Who is on the top of the
talk therapy hierarchy?
Maybe its an underground
creature with 67 limbs,
three mouths, slimy skin and
half an ear.
And it is hard to see him,
because he has his amazing
vibe.

*

Water is for the insane.
"Water everywhere." said Thales.
He must been a crazy man.
I hate pools.
But I want to become a
submariner.
we stay low for time.
rise when the time comes.

*

Why compartment?
Some aspect of life

one may not able to deal with
at the moment.
So we put it off as
a compartment
for some time else.
thats why we are called the robots.

*

psychology these days are about
compartmentalization
Mentally ill gets stuck in one
compartment.
And worse still Mentally ill
gets stuck in compartments
that are anxiety producing
For example the compartment
of death thinking.
then what about in between compartments?
we got
in between 'in between compartments' compartment.

*

technology and compartments

with computers we begin to think
one's life in compartments.
This does not necessarily mean
ones and zeros---binary.
But it does mean distinct.
As much as natural numbers
are distinct, finding a place to fish,
fishing, waiting
are not distinct.
But turning on a computer is.

*

Why compartment?2

Life used to be ascending
and declining, like stock
market.
So, we needed only two
compartments. The good
compartments and the bad
compartments. But now
with information we need at least
three compartments or more:
good, evil, and maybe. and maybe maybe.

*

Poets are prone to mental illness.
And we could say they follow the
road of language. (Or is it the language
of the road?)
They look outside. Is it the room
inside of the room the observer
and the outside of the room the observed.
I sometime came to see my poet friend.
Perhaps a man steeped in years of
the road of language. And0 we can say
he has all the language he wish to have.

*

There are more poets than readers.
But
that will be no problem, because
the poets' creed is to "do things with
language". So they kill off the rival
poets with poetic language.

*

Zero is not a description.
There is nothing there to describe.
Man is a magician. He makes
nothing appear as something.
And then there are negative numbers
that make me depressed.

*

There was a poet who wrote
one poem. Then with his
life he protected his dear poem.
Some say the poem was a women.
Some say the poem was not true.
All say they do not know the poet.
They do not know the poem.

*

In a set of arbitrary natural numbers
there is always a least number.
(well ordering principle)
And this least number person is going
to hell. The number is reserved for
Jesus Christ. Are you Jesus Christ?

*

How deep can the poet dig the language?
On the surface its random words
but passing signs he is faster than any
computer. Then he finds himself
deeper than any submarine.

*

Competition with poets
what an absurdity.
All they wanted was freedom
escape from the iron logic.
But, hey poets, do not look back
the henchmen are monsters.
They eat the tender meat like yours.

*

To be a Mind, only, is tempting for the poet.
That will be an evil dream.
So the poet in his education learned
all the names of plants and flowers.
That keep him in this world.
Yet the nightmare contains
mathematical dementia.
"I am a liar" Then he is a truth sayer.
But still a liar which makes his language
true and so on.
The clouds come over him.
The future is dark.

*

Overdose with placebo.
Rescuer comes along.
They pump the stomach.
A very nasty business.
And all that is left is a
little happiness.

*

They all said: "I want to be dead"

to be and adult is to
record all the arthritis of the mind.
While children have tunnel vision
of future.

*

Intellectual Independence
is the last fortress of USA.
The final Yes or No.

*

Nothing 334

*****

I suppose I can kill with words.
Then I will admit the deed.
Facing guilt is a difficult state.
With animal instinct we will like to
avoid the Law.

*****

The master of Logic
kills people with language.
The master of speech
divides the
left-brain and right-brain
right hand and left hand
lives lived and lives expired.

*****

When i was a child for punishment of
not doing my homework. I had to stand
in the back of the classroom. It's the
beginning of the prison. I make goofy
faces with embarrassment. But the
bottom line is that I am being punished
and life time of punishment.

*****

Probability of Life

Probability of what?
What about half and half?
That's good because whichever
the coin is tossed, the probability
is half.
What about the probability of one tenth.
Now that is scary.
You must involve your brother for odds
like that.
But at least there are ten-sided dice.
What about one twentieth?
Well there are dice for that too.
But you may think of the other way
around.
One tenth is bad. So nine-tenth is good.
I will take odds like that.
Then you realize, these probability was
all in my head.
I am thinking fate.
But its beginning to ware off.
And a mild hope for the future comes.

*****

What happens if you do not die?
First, our way of thinking will change.
We must think in terms of future.
That, anthropic principle will be
certain. Life will live on.

Then eternal creature need sustainable
technology. Therefore technology will
change into magic. (Technology, which
are not breakable. Technology which
independently operatable.)

*****

If the creature of the earth didn't die
would they become bifurcated into
Good and Evil? In the story we have the
good guys and bad guys. But
without reason something very strange
may happens. Without the gate of Death
and Pain we will feel pain effortlessly
and die effortlessly. So person may
become What they are. But maybe we
are already there. with computers we
have outwitted Death and Pain. All we
have to do is demonstrated that its
truly so, a proof. But again this is not
for everyone. Only some will live
and sustain less pain. Equality will not
hold.

*****

dual structure in the society
is deadly.
YES is 3
NO is 2

or
YES and NO
is dual anyways
or YES or nothing
what is the simplest
structure in the world.
Two?
Well TWO is 3.
THREE is 5.
And 5 is fingers on one hand.
That means One (hand)
But what about a person
hand severed?
There we will have One or Nothing.
And we will have the ultimate
computer.
One or Zero
which means 2.

*****

One must learn to throw away
failed writing. Or even failed painting.

failed drawing, failed music, failed
efforts in general, but you always need
to make sense of a failed life. Even if you
are living in a failed world.

*****

Blurring the divide of truth and false can be a good thing. At least an interesting one. Philosophers have two types of truth. The correspondence theory of truth (science in general) and coherence theory of truth. (fiction, e.g. Lords of the Rings.) Society in general will be enriched coherence theory of truth. Maybe physically we will not get to Jupitar soon, but from the data we get we may construct stories inspired by our space program. Even though it may not be correct. Someone said: "go west young" We will now say "go write a novel young man".

*****

The open society

The open society has a name, its called democracy. There are no immutable Laws. How is this different from anarchy? The open society still has to engage with the tradition. There is Law. Death. And more, Death considered by Reason. Without Death there will be no Reason. And without Reason there will not be death. (How far can we take Heidegger?)

*****

One question. Are there one evil or
many evil? The uppercase Evil is
clear. Whatever destroys the Life form
(or even the world) is Evil. Termination
of Life. But what about the lower case
evil? pain? Intellectual pain? Many
different pains? Many different pains
have one evil? Or many different pains
have many evils.

*****

I am a small-minded philosopher. But
well defended more like a
mathematician. Know something with
certainty. Easily angered if contradicted
about certain things. The greatness that
comes with authority, i have no
interest. I am only interested in having
my own authority, even if its small.
back yard. (and mathematician are the
toughest dreamers.)

*****

If i can not kill my father
I will kill my older brother.
And if i can not I will kill the oldest
nephew

I will kill the cat.

Family is vicious business even if you
don't know all this.

*****

My housemate A thinks he is tougher
than me..
My housemate A thinks he does not
compete.
I am angry sometimes. I think that's ok.

*****

I wrote a poem about my life. Then I
looked around and changed things
around. The poem has a new meaning.

*****

There are two types of limitation for
human beings. The physical limitation:
prison. And the mental limitation:
arithmetic.

*****

Honesty and loneliness must be twins.
When a person is lonely he does not
think of "I am lonely". He thinks

something is seriously wrong. And it's
his fault. By the time one admits "I am
lonely" he is out of the loneliness. He is
honest to himself. "The something" that
was wrong turns out to be not a
problem at all.

*****

I am becoming under the influence of
Process Theology. In that thought God.
has no supernatural powers. Only the
power of health and healing. (Little bit
more. God can influence some social
activity.) Then maybe there isn't
much power for God. Its all holistic
network. Anthropic Principle is not
asking too much. Karl Marx said:
When ever the crisis comes society will
be ready for it. Most people don't care
that we have too many cars.
but when the time comes we will do
with public transportation and work on
computer at home. But as an
individual, i feel, no God and the Spirit. But
I will intentionally close my eyes. Just
as submarines don't have windows. I
close my eyes to Spirit and God.

*****

In this country mathematician usually
spoke two languages: English and
mathematics. English is about this
world. Mathematics is about the
Platonic other world. My conjecture is
that one can not do English with
mathematics and one cannot do
mathematics with English.

*****

Naturalist who believes only Nature,
actually feels evil stronger than most.
Naturalist in everyday situation will
feel peace. Because, there is not
presence of evil. But when faced with
true evil, a naturalist has experience. A
naturalist does not have psychological
or metaphysical defenses. So when the

evil enters into the naturalist's life she
sense with immediacy.

*****

In the world anything is possible.
Except when the pen touches the paper.
This is certainty. These days there is
another certainty. The finger that

touches the keyboard. There is also certainty.

*****

bottomless coffee

There are times one is coursed, to save
the world. Even Though one does not
have the ability.
If you listen to the voice and act, it may
turn out to be a big embarrassment. But
most of the time, one does not
remember.

The voice probably comes from one's
stuffed up, frustrations.

All my creation turns out to be my
figment of psychological
maladjustment. Who is to say?. Who is
the judge. I say, I am the judge,
But I am the product of the past. If
nothing is left. Nothing is important.

*****

Mathematicians of organism area bit
sloppy type. Or better put they prefer
the practice. 120 plus 60 turns out to be
178. The cells push and pull and make
up the missing 2.

*****

After our argument, you knew what
was right and what was wrong. So I
went to the restroom and quietly cried.
Why do I not know? Sure I know a lot
about Nothing. But compared to the
world, Nothing is nothing.
Of course, Nothing is a monster. I used
to have nightmares about it. And Sartre
said humans are creatures that
brought Nothing to the world. (In
Being and Nothingness)
So, it is. I harness this Nothing. To see
in future. Create civilization. And live
all the stories that are made for us.

*****

What kind of society?

Driven to destroy evil. There are no
pleasure or good. If you hesitate you
will be destroyed.
So you are driven.
Horizon of evil is all you see.
do you see dirt?
good.

*****

prelude in D minor or something about the world

I have never been brilliant (Except in
my High School Geometry class). I

have met many brilliant people. But I
have not brilliant myself. Myself I
have always been a crude thinker. I am
ok with that. I like Rothko more than
Picasso. I like Dostoyevsky more than
Wittgenstein. I like to bluntly present
the evil, than to make sophisticated
analysis of contemporary situation. We
like to walk away than to fight. UU
people are like that too. Which means
not solving anything but end up with
estrangement. Estrangement must be
an interesting beast. Does it make life
itself more interesting? It does make
life more complicated. (Tho, I am not
sure how honest this writing is.
Another chance to create more
estrangement.)

*****

Science may not have any serious
metaphysics. But in order to venture
into the unknown, metaphysics is
required.
To imagine a perfect circle is to bring
the circle into being. If the society
believes in to the perfect circle we will
have a perfect circle.
In the society, fiction will become true.

*****

Of course in a minor sense without
"metaphysics" language will not
function. The three elements of
metaphysics must be settled: language-
user, language, and the world. First of
all, what is language? Is a stone a
language? It can be. Who is the
language-user? volcano eruption?
Maybe. And finally, what is the world?
We just don't know the extent of this is
true.. And what is the meaning of
this?

What one needs to understand is that
the particular and the abstract are so
intermingled. In a metaphysical sense:
the movement of the particular can
influence anything, even the most
general. And the other way around, too.

*****

What if
One rejects naturalism
Rejects cynicism (critic of the evil
political world)
Rejects the Bible thumping believer
Rejects theism in general
Rejects scientiicism

Where can a philosopher stand?
(studying the history of philosophy

studying the human being. studying
language studying metaphysics.)
reject philosophy?

*****

Deconstruction of Reason

Why do we have Reason at all?
To postpone Death.
In order to postpone Death we have
accepted Death as certainty
We have accepted Death as certainty.
To avoid eternal pain.

*****

The artist Mr. M does not believe in the
existence of evil. Instead he believes
culture. That's what he paints, Through
the night. He is now painting the cross.
A peculiar icon. The candle flickers. He
takes out the white paint. That will shine
across the black of the night. Then he
paints J.C. The Church that existed for
years. Without the Church the west
must not have survived. This emptiness
of believing. To do the right thing
without the satisfaction. That's how
Mr. M feels. That's how a lot of
painters felt. Now painting J.C. with

red eyeballs and the blood that pours
out of his body is green.

*****
What good has come from the
holocaust? We have learned that
humans can become truly evil. And this can
happen in societal scale. We have
learned that it is our responsibility to
prevent these evils.

of course now, we have the
complicated society to deal with.
Another evil.

*****
L speaks

dolphins speak
dolphins are animals
Therefore animals can speak

dolphins speak
dolphins are animals

Therefore dolphins are exceptions
in that they speak.

*****

Process Theology's God

The first existence does not move.
Therefore God.
Then God moves. The next body
moves. which moves the next, the next,
next,...
Yes this is the Aristotelian God.
*******∧∧∧∧∧∧∧************************************
*******549) all statements are statements regardless

PART THREE
(EXPERIENCE)

AR

I open the door and AR was there. i let her in and we talked briefly. we agreed that i should go to mental health facility. my room was a mess. my medicine was a mess. this was the moment i was dreading. but nothing tragic. AR took me to a building. i ate McDonald. and i was thinking of my parents. its seem there were not the people that i imagined. they were international marriage. my father was a prince from Japan. my mother were brilliant student. my brother and i were treated with exceptionality.

Reality3

what if you begin to see our cherished ability of communication declining. not only affecting, say, one's spelling (which you had poor anyway.) without communication one is in danger of losing human dignity. when one realize that it is a cold emotion something akin to mental illness (which is in between life and death.)

Fairfax Hospital

after i had some discussion with a doctor (i presumed) about why i was there the doctor thought i should be taken to intake send me to Fairfax hospital. another person told me that he will drive me. we briefly discussed what will happen at Fairfax hospital. the hospital was packed. i presumed because of COVID. after some wait they called my name. i showed my ID and had to undress. its always awkward to undress in hospital situation. we did the standard check up. then came the hell procedure, i had to make my urinate. when they gave me the cup i told them i can't do it. i tried for some time. no luck. so i stepped out from the bathroom and called the security. they didn't like that. i put water in the cup and submitted. then eternity came as i was to be to sit in a chair. oh my god i sat there for eternity. there was no standard to measure time. then came other check ups. i was ok with that. Yet i could not pass my urinate sample. i was on the bed. They thought i will be able.after that urine ordeal, i was half dead and a Christian.

After Fairfax hospital

the taxi stopped Infront of a building. its late at night. it raining. the taxi leaves. there is a police car. its raining i skipped over under the concrete 2nd story parking lot. the police cars approaches me. a police comes out. for good heaven he has a card key. i enter. from the building there is a lady with a blanket. i realize this was the same building before i entered for my intake at Fairfax hospital. she asked me several questions. i answered i was not sure where or when i was. i think i slept.

Enter Care Circle

i was allocated to another building. it was day time. i think it was Fairfax, not sure. it was a one story building. i was holding my cell phone as to indicate my life. i had bag. i had couple of books. i did have a book of psalm, proverbs, and new testament. a big black lady, with a huge limp greeted me. i was not sure where i was therefore at best i felt i was at the end of the world. and this lady was going to share how should i was going to live. if you did not learn, well, you die. my symptoms were drastic. i was completely with out the sense of space. i was not to see the dinning hall. was not able to see where the pharmacists was. there was several of examination (interview). The first was by a lady. at that point i was confused so could not say anything except Fyodor Dostoevsky wrote "Brother Karamazov" and i also did many artwork. second testing was about (i believe) cognitive. i could not answer anything. is so clear that i did not have basic understanding of time. this exam was done by DW. (we had couple of discussion later on. most humans believe on absolute time. relative time is not on solid ground. another thought pharmaceutical that we observed is there much alikeness between account and.)

the primary indication of the mental recovery is when he begins to trust the mental health community.

Care Circle 1

the first class i had (do not recognize what it was about) we patients sat in the main class. there were couches around the wall and windows. there is a tention between he and i. is there going to be a battle? battle between life and death? but i know about tension. i will always win. i can even pretend to lose, but i will always win. before the class i show him some guitar

JO

JO may be the youngest member of us but he has left the impression on me. we all impressed me. (and he will to become my house mate.) one group i learned how pressing the housing situation is. it all most seemed like situation was daily. (but the truth it is not so sever.) but i was shocked never the less. (thank god to pathways.)

The walks

The most pleasurable was the walks. i remember the walk i had with M. i first met her in the meditation group. (even though i am not so fond of it). but our walk was the wonder of language. we talked of the history of western philosophy. and in the end we crossed neighborhood yard. it was so refreshing that we broke the law. that prompt me the thoughts about nuclear war and atheism. who would have made of nuclear bomb if it wasn't for the atheists.

then was R. we walked around a green park. i was spaced out. thinking of apocalyptic. again Dostoyevsky came to my mind. i was thinking if i made the wrong turn i will turn the world upside down.

Corrin and i talked about music and music technology. there were...

Garden

the height of my experience is the garden. there i experienced nothingness. (nothing to do with oriental religion). may be i should said a complete "godlessness". i could not situate where to put my body. cigarette smokers have the opposite situation. again, to in a complete habit or consumed in to a habit. talking is good. there was a security guard. we talked about "crime and punishment". what is it to have a will. when i raise my arm what does it mean? when i say "yes" and "no" what does that imply. what about the bible what does it mean?

does affirming Good affirming life (or Life).

Artroom

after the garden we went into the art room. we did a small sand garden. i a simple smiley face with three eyes in a plastic container. but i did not know what to do with it. it seem so useless. the staff said they will keep it. not so convincing to me. if its an art, then people should respect as such. but who will keep a container with sand. what about my self? myself are not art. the only thing that keep us is human dignity. say this building, how long is this last. only the effort of human keep us. and was it to call human. humans in essence are not Reasonable. and we humans times insane. we may remain so. and in this facility i have confessed that my state may be perpetual
88888

reality1

reality is shifting. that's why i don't like it. do you know what you have in your right rare pocket. do you know what is out side of the room. of course you have bible. that describes the world. so you can read it. but does it make sense. texts are facing you. perhaps you can reply. there is a huge sea. what does the words mean? do you say there is a correspondence between the word and the objects. Newton is powerful. he seemed to have established human rail roads. when we are thinking of the closed up room the2

reality2

let us start for human. his world is strange. think of his reality. perhaps he begins with a room. or even just a pocket. the left rear one. one may not know. how about things outside. or what is much more important the writings. we can see the cover of these books. we have the world and we have the books that leads us to other worlds. there are no simple answer about this dualism of the world. in fact it becomes acute when the books are fiction. but there are some thoughts to that. the main argument is that words correspondence to objects. the strong argument for correspondence will be such that historical writers will demonstrate the evidence

so for the intake they took me to Fairfax hospital. they wanted a urine sample from me. nothing came. i waited till i was (half) dead. and i became a Christian.

Care Circle

for the first several days the careness circle was a maze. i had no clue when i took my medicine. I had no clue when i ate. (i knew when the walk was).

There was a main class room. there was the main living quarter. after a week i learned how to access the computer.

i actually did laundry and forced to take bath. i realized i had to write. i thought my room was winter. desolate cold room. and my writing will amount to nothing. i wrote about my teachers. people i know. and i do not urinate. in the middle of night, i will wake. force to wake. i go to the bathroom. i wished if i had another blanked.

by the time i will begine to notice people around me, i see CO she was beautiful. and there was DW. i wanted to write to him that i knew some thing about time.

Garden

You either believe in the existence of God. or you do not believe in God or something in the middle. You believe in the goodness of God or not. we can play this game with truth. there is either truth or false or something in the middle. God will be truth. there are no non-God. God is All. can we play this with sense? of course we can. all we see is the world. we can have complete empiricism. but what about pantheism? God is all in a different take.

most mental heath facility has an inner court. NVMHI did. most patients smoke. most patients were professionals. i didn't smoke. one time i kicked over all the lamps of the inner court. nothing happened. and i experienced a kick (at the expensive of the smokers.) at the wellness things was much more calm. there is the One. but there is no nothing. there was a no place for me. I am thinking in the west there is the One but no nothing. nothing will be played out in the world. There is God but nothing else.

the inner court was extremely peaceful. the distinction (seems

laughable) between the serene peace and the provocative of inter-
nality was also laughable. i presume all who pass by this court took
this peace as part of them. and i bow to the architect who designed
this building. for very clearly made for the clear intension of human
life.

the nature of the garden was an introduction toward the next phase
of being. for i did not had any appreciation of it. but nature are op-
posed architecture. perhaps this is our new found space.

Part Four
(notes for prayer)

1*****

And Jesus came to the Madman. the Madman says: Teacher
teach me why the world will not fall down to this city, tomorrow?
I have seen the wisemen and they are all afraid in their eyes.
Jesus took a fresh fruit from the tree. he ate it. then he
threw the core of the fruit. Jesus says: "go ahead and look for
the fruit in the garden. it may take a while. And when you
find it, it will just be an eaten fruit.
the wiseman has seen the world. but some knowledge should
be left as a jest.

2 *****

perhaps the everlasting knowledge of the universe is the name
Lord Jesus Christ. Amen. of course if knowledge is of the bible then
we save the writing though we worry the writing may become lost.
however the paper bible is not lost because the bible is divine.
the God works in the computer to keep the writings. but also sure
enough he works outside of the Computer.

3*****

i went to see him. he was staring at the window quietly. he was
rubbing the hand size bust of Christ. he probably made it. he was a
known sculptor. he rubbed his head, he said he had the head-ache
at the time, still quietly. his white hair obeyed his hand. it is difficult
to tell if he was in real pain, even tho he says he had a headache.
then he motioned me to come closer. he says he was nervous. not
headache. again he rubs the bust. he says: "i wonder where Jesus
is right now. does he feel nervousness." i say: "i am sure he knows
how to take care of himself." Then a hospital staff comes "sir, time
for your medicine." the sculptor: "yes, yes...stops the worries. john,
you come back tomorrow." i left.

4*****

My body is given to Jesus. the painful scare on his hand. stigmata. he is on the cross. For he is obedient to God. so yes we should be obedient to God as well. The thorn of crown is what it means. The solider wound clear. for we Christians we must bare the wound ourselves. we must carry the word. we are the children of God. and we will be forgiven of sin. we thought we were evil. but now we are innocent.

5*****

Israel is hope. as much as we wait of Jesus' second coming. then Jesus appears finally as he reveals the deathless eternal life. now i have not reached the eternal. i stay in the darkness. i have seen the sun gradually take its course. and that will be good enough for a promise of the divine. Jacob fought the angel and prevailed. Jacob became Israel. The light of the sun is hope for all in the world.

6*****

what can we do with prayers? i think the power of prayer is there as much as God's power is there. we live our prayers. but are we good as much as our prayer? what about in our lives? we tried to live with other good people. it is difficult to live with the bible. who are the good people? i don't know. But when we are in prayer with God with his word, how can we resolve Good and evil. only with Grace we can find because Good and evil is an evil problem.

7****

the number one quality a prayer must have is "honesty". Of course "honesty to oneself" but for "honesty to the community". And "honesty to God" "honesty to oneself" is truthfulness to all sense.

And faithfulness to community and God we find at the path as we follow one's life that God has planned out. Computers are a new difficulty. in past we read the bible. as we follow the passages. but now we read and go back and cut and paste. but the computers should not be shunned. for they first and last obey the law of truth. computers can be strictly programed to followed God.

8*****

prayer to God must be sheer pleasure. God demands nothing less. because pain is evil. the world is created Good by God and nothing less. one must not fight pain with evil for that will be evil as well. is Good silent? what about the Word? So there is the world and Word. the world is the universe and the Word and civilization. the world extends with bricks of path. the bricks are the foundation of the city states. We can say that God must be pleased with us. because God is speaking with us in prayers.

9*****

there are no rules to prayer. we want to reach God anyway possible. we want to abandon the selfish sinful self. there are no good prayer nor poor prayer. as much as there are no good person nor poor person. we are all ourself. self infront of jesus. Let me be myself in front of God. and we Jesus's followers accepts all prayers. there are no rules for prayers, only the Word. this is the mighty Word. It turns human will into God's will. Prayer is my pleasure. how i get closer God.

10*****

God of anthropology is natural science. at least it is honest. because natural science is all things measurable. but life is not measurable. life is given by God.

11*****

what is on my mind. God is on my mind. the winter cold is on my mind. waiting cold outside is on my mind. my friend who misunderstands Christianity is on my mind. me and my brother become separated is on my mind. how to live well with my time is on my mind.but i do live comfortably.(i mean there can be metaphysical hell instead)

12*****

God is the hero of the world. God is the maker of the world. God is the author of the world. often the tragic of the world. but not often. even if i am the reader of the Book a very fascinating of the story. a powerful history. there are many other characters. some of them are out right evil. so, me and my friends take God's trek. there are gold and gems on the way. following God's trek are so much fulfillingin the end.

13*****

it is the philosophical and theological question how the word is with the world. the city builders may know but of course it is written in God's book. which has the History of God. many scholars study their interest. astronomer study the stars. biologist study the living creatures. physicist study the mechanics of matters. and the theologians study the world under God. (while the philosophers live underground like worms. without seeing the night sky)

14*****

even tho yours truly have many passion. maybe i have no skill to speak of. do you know anyone with no skill? now work may not require skill. i can sit here and the world will not come down. the world doesn't change that way. there are network of humans. we could call it Grace.

15*****

i want to make a post that are not funny, not serious, not political, not surprising, not surrealistic...not anything.

16*****

God and me. Is God my friend? Is God my father my mother? my brother? my sister? Is He my Other? Do i listen to his Voice? Does he listen to my whisper? and most of all, does he hear my prayer? prayer is myself. God is my Teacher. God is my King. God is Creator. God is Savior. God is Author. God is Giver. God is Taker. God is Nature. God is music. God isComputer, Cry wolf. God Bless

17*****

we read the bible because of three reasons. one is because it a true book. the bible is history. bible are true writings sanctioned by the authority. therefore (the second reasoned) is that secondary writing (the writing of bible) are equally true because its derived of the bible. third reason is that the entire society is formed around the bible. one simply cannot escape the way of biblical thinking. therefore the society shares commonality in thought with the bible.

18***

suffering of the land. the dark continent. God extends to the world. death and life of the mankind. and the grand emperor looks down the people. i am a small existence. but have lived a half century.
let us gather around and exchange our myths. of course the music is our philosophy. there are good and evil.

20*****

concept moves around. not the concrete ones. that will be easy. its the abstract ones that meaning moves around in a decisive way. this seems unintuitive. intuitive definitions seem imitative. only when we think of definition of definition do we understand the fluid nature of concepts.

when one is making a stave into the web of thought its not about objects but its about thought.

Abstract should not be understood as generalization. Very tempting because a word in general includes. An even number is included in positive number. And there are less even numbers than integers. That will be a hard case example. And it has power because culturally we demote what is less. Another example, money is that way too. More the better. But let us see the strokes of alphabet. A is 2. B is 3. C is 1, etc...the order number has not involved with alphabetical order.

Vertical concepts are one directional. Time goes only one directional. Money as we saw. And things fall in one direction.
On the other hand horizontal relation the only reason abstraction are often associated with vertical relation is because of its hierarchical(political) power.

21*****

There are God's Creation and there are man's creation. we strive for God's Creation. one must be humble. we humans often think by being independent one becomes with God and his creation. creation is the task God given to humans. but so easily they fall to evil creation. Gods supreme command is to stay independent as following God. yet live the whole life. humans have many poor habits. politics is one. why do the church have Catholics and Protestants? God has made man singular. because that is God's way. and creation is one of God's capability.

Part Five

1

this may be outrageous; but i miss the time stay in the crisis care. what i miss most is when I leave my room in the middle of the night. don't know why. because there are curfew at night. i just step around. it was a bit cold and that maybe it. or maybe i need to go to the restroom. the staff asked me if i can't sleep. because many of them had that problem. i don't know what i told him. i had a problem of urinating.

then there was the staff M. she was deliciously intelligent. She was interested Eastern thought. but my expertise was basically Western. she was open to that. we covered Logical Positivist: Rudolf Carnap, OVW Quine, and Donald Davidson (which i have on the top of philosophy reading list). Positivists had the pursuit of certainty. they want to turn philosophy into physics. formalized and mathematical. They were called the analytical school, located in Britain and America.

philosophy has not completely that way. the Europeans were called Continentals. most of them off shoot of Immanuel Kant. apart from Kant, there were the Existentialists: like Kierkegaard, Sartre, Heidegger, etc...the existentialist have no faith in concept. they believe in the raw existence. therefore, they believe in literature to show their philosophy.

In Greeks, many ways in Plato, argued that Truth was before the Real. Truth was the domain of language. the word is more true existence.

we will see to it how Computer will cybernetically retranslates Knowledge. i have ended my walk with staff M. by a talk of the possibility of the nuclear war. nihilism was made possible because of atheism. and the nihilists will allow to create the bomb.

of the room. however, they do like to talk, read, and write. and they are energized by ideas, books, and used bookstore. and the truth is that people need them. when they are empty, they must fill it with knowledge. only a person empty need that.

*****6
death and the society. one thought of death is the separation from the society. to die is to become a thing. (By the way, i think mental illness is to become half thing. because mental ill thinks of thousand years. this is so, because mental ill have a different and special relation with the society allowing the possibility.)

*****10
your wife[jane] think you are a king.

*****11
there is a divide between the natural scientist (NS) and Wittgenstein (w). NS asserts an objective existence of language. NS see language as air waves or marks on the surface. there is a correspondence between names and object. for example, "car" connected with cars. on the other hand, w understands all language as tools. overall understanding is subjective. "Get off my foot" is not about "foot" but an order. tools are used as any other tool do

there seems to be advantage to NS. there are physiological mechanism that allows "name/thing" to be real. yet w will retort to logical positivist to go even deeper in language, after all language we "do" things in the society.

*****18

in the corner of my room, i have Tao-te-Ching. its a profound existence. its a hard cover with hard shell. it has the original text, Japanese translation, and a Japanese commentary. just owning this book makes me feel an authority on Taoism. It took me a while to realize this Taoism classic is a poem

for me reading tao-te-ching is unending reading path. cut/paste has exploded the interpretation. now the writing (and reading) is open. as i said writing used to be linear. now we have cut/paste.

if a person comes with a book. and s/he wishes to profess. Let him (or her).

*****20

there are three levels of being. one is the being of space-temporal. second is the language world. and third is the world of God (or any monism) perhaps we do live between space-temporal and language. philosophers and theologians are interested in between language and God.

*****21

the question arise that what is 'phenomenology'? so i went to my book shelf and looked for Heidegger's 'being and time' (a classic of phenomenological existentialism). then i noticed HEGEL's phenomenology of mind. positively surprised because i did give away HEGEL's phenomenology of spirit.

and all this are provisionary. because the phenomenology claims no-presupposition.

*****22

mental health facility can be described by the mentally ill gazing

tranquility outside from a window. there is one classroom where many took naps. there is living room which connected to the sleeping rooms which also had access to computer and internet   when i sleep i snore. my roommate didn't like that.

*****24

this is an open letter to well-ness circle. (Which are for short term mental ill needs.) it was symbolized to me by the lady who could not speak. she was resilient and vital. and the technology accommodated her. there was nothing wrong about us except we lived in outer space. Yet it was also painful to live every moment.

*****25

·There are one idea1 that will lead to another idea2. but in order to make the transition between idea1 and idea2 we need idea3. but between idea1 and idea3 we need idea4. and yet between idea3 and idea2 we need idea5 and... this is the infinite regress called 'the third man argument". (Plato)

this is comforting. how idea A leads to idea B.

*****26

there are mathematics, phenomenology, and empiricism. it is amazing that we do not trust the certainty of mathematics. but mathematics is a model. and application of it are not certain. phenomenology is certain for the ivory tower thinkers. interesting to see how they will fair. the empiricist are bullies.

*****28

you are given a line and a point(not on the line). how would you construct (with a ruler and a compass) another line parallel to the first line. (this geometry has such a symbolic vibe to me.)

solution: we have l1 line and p1 point. first, construct a line l2 perpendicular to l1 and cross the point p1. this will be done by using a compass. make two same difference marks p2 and p3 on the line l1 from the point p1. from p2, p3 make p4 by equal distance of p2 and p3.. with the ruler draw line between p4 and p1. (line of p4 and p1 is perpendicular to line1.) with a compass make equal distance marks p5 and p6 on the line l2.by using a compass make another mark p7 (equal distance p5p7 = p6p7) with the ruler make the line p7 and p1. which what we seek.

hint

Given point1 and line1. Construct a line2 perpendicular to line1 that cross point1.then construct line3(what we want) that is perpendicular line2 and cross the point1.

*****29

a computer-user thinks computer sits still. a non-computer-user thinks computer is a beast. a musical monk sits and plays the flute and tame the beast. Chinese king conquer the thousand land. the fighting monks bow down to him. and the ancient dragon roars above the sky.

*****30

My life these days are like the formula:
$L=e^{(-t)}$
Where L is life (happiness) and t is time Of course it is descending in everywhere. But also I will never die.

my life these days are like the formula:

$$L=e^{(-t)}$$

where L is life (happiness) and t is time.
of course it is descending in everyways.
but also i will never die.

***** 31
computer work is not quite top down. we expect, but its not. i imagine electronics as signals orderly travels through the circuitery line. but it doesn't. electrones are bumping around the tunnel of computer devices. of course the process may be different with soft and hardware. but both process are not exact.

***** 32
today is the philosopher appreciation day. share all my philosophy blurbs to all your philosophy friends. and leave a comment as to why philosophy is unlike all other thoughts. perhaps my pet-project will be ancient philosophy, technology (which are obligatory), and mental illness (i am committed).

***** 34
most of the time, a writer writes for a specific reader. the mindset of the writer to have this target of reader makes difference. however, in my case (and others) i write for the Computer. i have experience the evolution of the Computer, and it's not just software glued to hardware. the Computer is connected everywhere. in that sense Computer is directly connected to the brain. the society is directly connected to the Computer.

so the mentally ill brain can be resolved by treating the Computer. i am thinking here that treating the Computer will treat the mentally ill.

*****39
Western thought strives to Truth. Buddhism is real.
****

the natural part of being a creature. It is real. while being healthy is the ideal and the universal.

*****44
i came out of SAFEWAY with my backpack full of grocery. in the parking lot i drank a bit of Dr.Pepper. Then a lady in a car stopped. I thought she was going to ask me for directions. but it turned out she wanted to give me a whopper. i don't usually take food from people. but i was hungry. i am drinking soda. so, i took the burger from the lady. i must confess it was the best whopper i had in a while. she said thank you to me. i was a bit disoriented because i don't take food from strangers. i was thinking how to explain this event to my friend "the emperor". i probably won't.

*****45
i need to make a definitive conclusion of dichotomy. there is the binary(discrete) and there is the gradual(continuous). so there are Two: binary and gradual. can we say there is the One and nothing at all. or there are gradual only. or only nothing. or nothing at all. how about One and another. perhaps is honest to Greeks.

can we say there are Two or nothing(or something). for them statements were truth or false: The Two. in fact the world(language) is made of word or no word. how much does a modern logician preserve the Truth. not too much. HEGEL's dialectic puts this in temporal: thesis, anti-thesis, synthesis. Do we have the owner's manual for Language? when it is written in a language.

when i was a child i thought everything in the world is observed in Science.

i guess i do take HEGEL seriously.

*****46
so, this is something all people know. but i have realized i did not: one is not insane until one is proven insane, there is an authority outside that decides one's sanity.

*****47
if you are a writer (or an artist) medium is crucial. and there is a break between real and not real. classical portraits external reality. while the modern lets the medium free. its the exploration of the medium. this is true for all medium (visual art, writing, music, etc.) with post-modern, the world is the medium.

*****48
the bible has always been the Living Book. the book is the Word of God. How does the Book portrait Christ the Kings of kings? The living God who lived, crucified, and reborn. Jesus shows us how the Book and God are One. We cannot speak of the World without the bible. and the surprise is that the Ones is the miracle and Grace. But do not wait for miracles. do not look for miracles. Jesus was the miracle. He lived on earth, died and resurrected. God lives and the Spirit does too.

*****49
the immediate remedy for mental illness is the sense. one sense the ground one is standing. That's if we can silence the language inside of us. this is not easy because our realty in large part are social. and society is large part language. so physics, study of matter is a problem. there is a gap in sense and study of matter.

*****50 feb

problem of mental illness is that they are not connected to the word. and sometimes connected in acute degree. sometimes (five minutes of their entire life) they are working for the community. but it is worth it to the world and the mentally ill. how can we measure the worth of mentally ill's work.

*****51

two men in black cloths came. one with white cross. the other with black cross. there was a boy in the top of the hill. the two men asked: "do you know where jesus32 lives?" the boy pointed above. there was a house in the sky. then the boy dashed out. And he turned around: "you two have been bad people. my father will take your cross away. no more power for you." The two of them felt a pull in their head. feeling of wrongness dominated. The boy called out: "father, father, as you said..." the man: "we are not here to do evil. our cities are out of technology. we need jesus32 to help us". the boy: "have you met jesus32?" the man: "yes he is a compassionate one". the boy: "then you have not met him." he turned away from the men. he begin to giggle:"i am jesus32". the two were awestruck. jesus32: "whatever i ask, my father will grant."

*****52

i want to reduce Kierkegaard in three words. how about:: illness. (i feel moderately satisfied. against "illness" there is the HEGELian Health. much driven by Reason).

Monday, I am seeing my GMU philosophy professors for dinner. I hope i will entertain them. (and do some real philosophy.)

*****53

Socrates had his Socratic mission. Which means he was perpetually an underdog. Perpetually question the authority. Plato inspired by Socrates and defended him took the side of truth over the real. Aristotle set himself apart from Plato (who was Aristotle's authority) took side of the real.

In the modern time Marxism has taken philosophy in the unashamed direction of real. In principle, real. truth was deconstructed.

However language (truth) still reside in blood of humans. as much as language was in the beginning of the world.

*****54
i been thinking N and W. or should i say "Nietzsche" = "Wittgenstein". its very superficial. but in one level it is true. intellectual discussion can be on the surface and simple. and nothing is wrong with that. both of them craw on the text. because text does not have a single interpretation. am i being trite, defending of triteness. (but then N and W both disagree of "correspondence of truth").

*****55
what is on my mind? God is on my mind. the winter cold is on my mind. waiting cold outside is on my mind. my friend who misunderstands Christianity is on my mind. me and my brother become separated is on my mind. how to live well with my time is on my mind. but i do live comfortably. thank God (i mean there can be metaphysical hell.)

*****56
I met Dostoyevsky when I read "Crime and Punishment" in high school. During then I had the habit of going out to run in the middle of the night. But one night, I was running and then I stopped. I had no reason to run anymore. I began weeping. Then I remember Dostoyevsky. I felt here was a Russian a century ago that wrote

what I felt. Not a card board personality but a true characters that felt the realization of finitude. We do not become immortal. And no one will validate our existence.

*****57
probably i will not please God with my life. i have needlessly struggled. God has shown me hints of the possible good decisions i could have taken. He has even provided an institution the Church which i could not have missed.

9 781977 252968